Takekuni Hirayoshi
Piano Works

ハバネラ
Habanera
ピアノ・ソロ　*for Piano Solo*
ピアノ連弾のための　*for Piano 4-Hands*

サンバ・カンシオン
Samba Canción
ピアノ・ソロ　*for Piano Solo*
ピアノ連弾のための　*for Piano 4-Hands*
クラリネットとピアノのための　*for Clarinet in B♭ and Piano*

初恋
The first love
バリトン、ヴァイオリン、ピアノ連弾のための
for Baritone, Violin, Piano 4-Hands
北原白秋　詩
poem by Hakushu Kitahara

〈平吉毅州遺作集〉

平吉毅州
作曲

edition KAWAI

皆様へのお願い

楽譜や歌詞・音楽書などの出版物を権利者に無断で複製（コピー）することは、著作権の侵害（私的利用など特別な場合を除く）にあたり、著作権法により罰せられます。また、出版物からの不法なコピーが行われますと、出版社は正常な出版活動が困難となり、ついには皆様方が必要とされるものも出版できなくなります。
音楽出版社と日本音楽著作権協会（JASRAC）は、著作者の権利を守り、なおいっそう優れた作品の出版普及に全力をあげて努力してまいります。どうか不法コピーの防止に、皆様方のご協力をお願い申しあげます。

カワイ出版
一般社団法人　日本音楽著作権協会

この曲集について

　ハバネラ（Habanera）は、1995年にピアノ・ソロ作品として作曲され、作曲者自らにより
ピアノ連弾作品に編曲されました。
　サンバ・カンシオン（Samba Canción）は、1992年にピアノ・ソロ作品として作曲され、同
じく作曲者自らによりピアノ連弾作品およびクラリネットとピアノ作品に編曲されました。
　Samba Canciónはスペイン語で、アルゼンチンの民謡の形を用いた小品で、8分の6拍子と4
分の3拍子が一緒になっています。たとえば、ピアノ・ソロ作品では、右手が8分の6拍子で
左手が4分の3拍子の形態で作曲されています。
　この2曲は作曲年が前後していますが、作曲者より、2曲続けて演奏するときは、ハバネラ、
サンバ・カンシオンの順で演奏するよう指示があります。

　「初　恋〜バリトン、ヴァイオリン、ピアノ連弾のための」は、1997年暮れに第21回 岩崎 淑
「ミュージック・イン・スタイル」委嘱作品として作曲されました。
　作曲者はこの作品に「白秋の抒情小曲集の中の一篇、＜初戀＞は、私の少年時代からずっ
とからだのどこかに居ついていた小品です。」というコメントを記しています。

カワイ出版

On this collection of music

"Habanera" was first composed in 1995 for piano solo, but later it was arranged into that for piano 4-hands by the composer himself.

"Samba Canción" was composed in 1992 for piano solo also, but was arranged later by the same composer into one for piano 4-hands and another for the clarinet and the piano.

"Samba Canción" is Spanish. It's a little music piece which employs Argentine folksongs. The tempo is of both 6/8 time and 3/4 time. For example, in the piano solo music piece, it's composed in such a way as the right hand playing in 6/8 time, but the left hand playing in 3/4 time.

These two pieces were written almost at the same time. However, it's so indicated that when two pieces are played on the same occasion, "Samba Canción" should be followed by "Habanera".

"The first love~for baritone, violin, piano 4-hands" was written towards the end of 1997, commissioned by the Shuku Iwasaki "Music in Style" 1997.

The writer said that "The first love" was one of Kitahara Hakushu's collections of lyrical poems and that the piece had been with him all through his childhood days.

edition KAWAI

もくじ／Contents

ハバネラ ピアノ・ソロ
Habanera for Piano Solo ———————————————————— 7

サンバ・カンシオン ピアノ・ソロ
Samba Canción for Piano Solo ———————————————— 10

ハバネラ ピアノ連弾のための
Habanera for Piano 4-Hands ——————————————————— 15

サンバ・カンシオン ピアノ連弾のための
Samba Canción for Piano 4-Hands ———————————————— 20

サンバ・カンシオン クラリネットとピアノのための
Samba Canción for Clarinet in B♭ and Piano ———————— 28

初 恋 バリトン、ヴァイオリン、ピアノ連弾のための
The first love for Baritone, Violin, Piano 4-Hands ————— 36

ハバネラ
Habanera
ピアノ・ソロ *for Piano Solo*
ピアノ連弾のための *for Piano 4-Hands*

サンバ・カンシオン
Samba Canción
ピアノ・ソロ *for Piano Solo*
ピアノ連弾のための *for Piano 4-Hands*
クラリネットとピアノのための *for Clarinet in B♭ and Piano*

＜作曲データ＞

ハバネラ　ピアノ・ソロ
作　　曲：1995年12月12日

サンバ・カンシオン　ピアノ・ソロ
作　　曲：1992年11月2日

ハバネラ　ピアノ連弾のための
作・編曲：1996年7月18日

サンバ・カンシオン　ピアノ連弾のための
作・編曲：1993年11月24日

サンバ・カンシオン　クラリネットとピアノのための
作・編曲：1996年7月14日

ハバネラ
Habanera

ピアノ・ソロ
for Piano Solo

平吉毅州 作曲
Takekuni Hirayoshi

© 1999 by edition KAWAI. Assigned 2017 to Zen-On Music Co., Ltd.

サンバ・カンシオン
Samba Canción

ピアノ・ソロ
for Piano Solo

平吉毅州 作曲
Takekuni Hirayoshi

★メトロノーム表示は、作曲者により左手を基準に表示してあります。
© 1999 by edition KAWAI. Assigned 2017 to Zen-On Music Co., Ltd.

＜ハバネラ　ピアノ・ソロ　作曲者自筆譜より＞　　＜サンバ・カンシオン　ピアノ・ソロ　作曲者自筆譜より＞

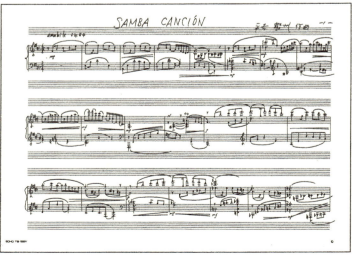

ハバネラ
Habanera

ピアノ連弾のための
for Piano 4-Hands

平吉毅州 作・編曲
Takekuni Hirayoshi

© 1999 by edition KAWAI. Assigned 2017 to Zen-On Music Co., Ltd.

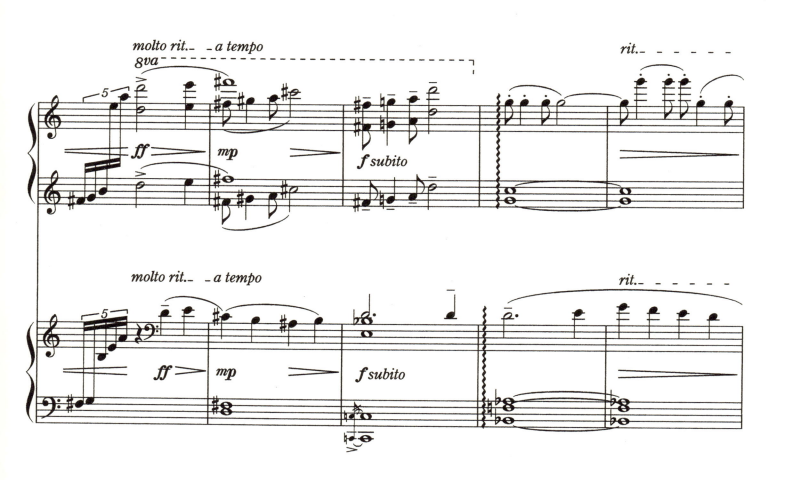

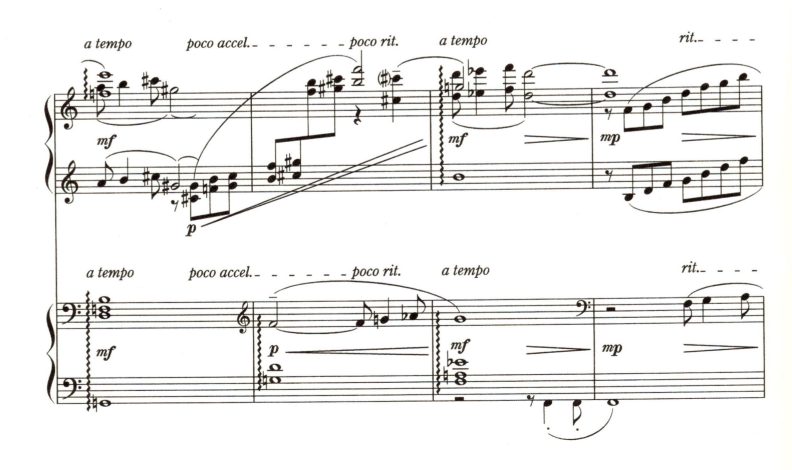

19

サンバ・カンシオン
Samba Canción

ピアノ連弾のための
for Piano 4-Hands

平吉毅州 作・編曲
Takekuni Hirayoshi

★メトロノーム表示は、作曲者によりセカンド・パートを基準に表示してあります。

© 1999 by edition KAWAI. Assigned 2017 to Zen-On Music Co., Ltd.

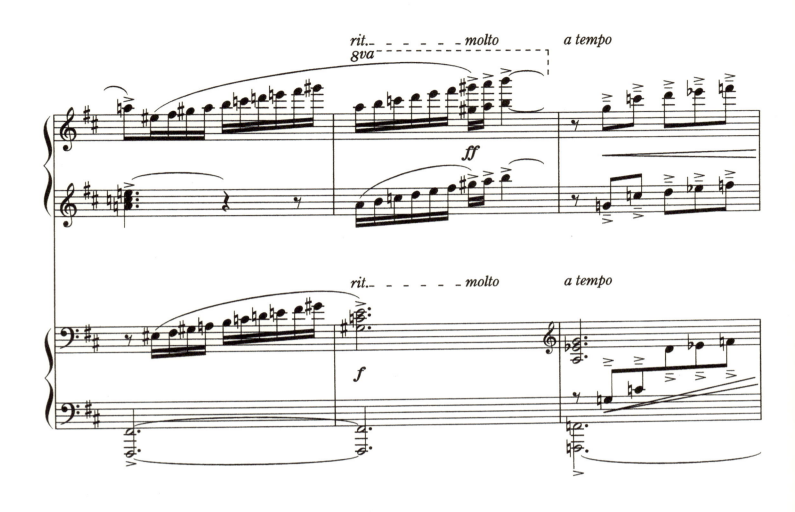

25

サンバ・カンシオン
Samba Canción

クラリネットとピアノのための
for Clarinet in B♭ and Piano

平吉毅州 作・編曲
Takekuni Hirayoshi

★メトロノーム表示は、作曲者によりピアノ・パートを基準に表示してあります。

© 1999 by edition KAWAI. Assigned 2017 to Zen-On Music Co., Ltd.

★から★★までのフレーズは1オクターヴ下げて演奏してもよい。

この作品のこと…

　桐朋学園大学に一週一度教えに行っている私は、時折お目にかかる平吉先生といつも音楽のこと、学生のことを親しくお話させていただいていた。

　「先生、ぜひ今年の私の〈ミュージック・イン・スタイル〉シリーズ・コンサートに作品をお書きいただけませんか？」

　10年程前にお願いした時、学校がとても忙しくて今は無理とおっしゃったので、一昨年定年退職され、沖縄県立芸術大学へ赴任されたのをきっかけに、今度は少しお時間があるのではないかと思って、再びお願いしたのは1997年春だった。沖縄は「ムーンビーチ・ミュージック・キャンプ＆フェスティバル」で18年間も行っている土地だし、沖縄でもお会いできればと私の心は高鳴っていた。「いいですよ。」と早速お返事をいただき、曲の編成を申し上げたら、「うーん、珍しい組合せだね。歌手の音域を聞いてください。」といわれた。

　こうして、ノルウェー王国芸術祭参加「ノルウェー音楽の夕べ」のタイトルのもと、第6回目から続けてきた邦人作曲家への委嘱作品として、平吉先生に曲を書いていただけることとなった。

　ノルウェーの作曲家の作品を中心にした歌曲、グリーグのヴァイオリン・ソナタ、ペールギュント組曲をピアノ連弾で弾くというプログラムなので、新曲はバリトン歌手、ヴァイオリン、ピアノ連弾のための作品となった。

　ノルウェーのバス・バリトン歌手、ニョール・スパルボ氏とはオスロで共演したことがあり、その時、日本の歌を巧みな日本語で歌われたので、彼を中心にプログラムを組むことにした。

　スパルボ氏の好意で、ノルウェーの作曲家ハッベスタ氏にも作品を委嘱した。平吉先生の11月8日付のお葉書には、「作品が遅れに遅れて申訳ありません。詩は北原白秋の〈初戀〉という抒情短詩です。歌のパートはうんと易しい旋律線となっています。あと、三、四日は、時間を下さいませんか。よろしくお願い申し上げます。」

　こうして、スパルボ氏到着2週間前に平吉先生の作品は届いた。北原白秋の詩、それは先生が初期の作品からよく使われた詩で、奇しくもこの委嘱作品が絶筆となられたと聞いて、白秋への想いの深さを改めて感じた。リハーサルにいらしていただけず、お電話で打ち合わせをした時、ヴァイオリンのパートがむずかしいと云われなかったかと心配された。しかし、新垣裕子さんは、すばらしい彼女の感性を発揮して見事に弾かれた。

　東京公演が終わった時、大きな拍手の中で先生をステージへお招きしたが、先生は立ち上がったまま、笑顔で私達の方を向いて拍手された、あのすてきな笑顔を今でも忘れない。

　平吉先生があの日を境に病に臥せられ、そして亡くなられたという事は、今もって信じがたい。先生のすばらしいこの作品を多くの方々が演奏されることを祈っている。

1999年2月

ピアニスト　岩崎　淑

＜作曲・初演データ＞

作　　曲：1997年11月16日

委　　嘱：第21回 岩崎 淑「ミュージック・イン・スタイル」
　　　　　Commissioned by the Shuku Iwasaki "Music in Style" 1997
　　　　　（ノルウェー王国芸術祭参加作品）

演奏初演：1997年12月2日／福岡市・福岡銀行本店大ホール
　　　　　1997年12月3日／広島県川尻町・ベイノロホール
　　　　　1997年12月4日／倉敷市・大原美術館　第65回 ギャラリーコンサート
　　　　　1997年12月5日／東京・サントリーホール小ホール
　　　　　1997年12月6日／天童市・天童市市民プラザ
　　　　　1997年12月7日／鶴岡市・中央公民館市民ホール

演　　奏：ニョール・スパルボ（バス・バリトン）　Njål Sparbo, Bass-baritone
　　　　　新垣裕子（ヴァイオリン）　Yuko Aragaki, Violin
　　　　　中村伸吾、岩崎　淑（ピアノ）　Shingo Nakamura, Shuku Iwasaki, Piano

On this music piece···

I used to enjoy discussions on music and students with Prof. Takekuni Hirayoshi whenever I saw him at the Tohoh Gakuen University of Music. Even now, I go to teach there once a week.

Almost a decade ago, I asked him to write a music piece for my serial concerts titled "Music in Style". But then he was terribly busy with his own work at school and he declined my request.

I again made the same request to Prof. Hirayoshi in the spring of 1997, as I heard he had retired a couple of years ago and that he was employed at the Okinawa Prefectural University of Arts. I thought, "Now is the high time for me to make a request to him, as he might be able to find time for it."

Talking of Okinawa, I have visited there for 18 times to hold the Moon Beach Music Camp and Festival and so I thought I might be able to meet him in Okinawa next time I go there. The thought made my heart throb with expectations.

When I met him there, he immediately okayed my request. When I told him about the contents of the music, he said, "Hm... quite a rare combination, isn't it? Now, tell me about the voice range of the singer."

Prof. Hirayoshi wrote this music piece for the "Visions of Norway 1997-1998" on the subject of "An Evening of Norweagian Music" at last, as a music piece by a Japanese composer.

I have been commissioning Japanese composers to write music pieces for the "Moon Beach Music Camp and Festival" ever since its 6th festival.

This programme consists mainly of works by Norwegian composers: Songs, Grieg's Sonata No.3 in C minor Op.45 and Peer Gynt's Suite No.1 Op.46 for Piano 4-hands, played by a baritone, a violinist and two pianists, respectively.

I once performed with the Norwegian bass-baritone, Njål Sparbo in Oslo. At the time, he sang some Japanese songs in Japanese. He was so impressive that I decided to include him in this programme.

In his favour, I commissioned a Norwegian composer, Kjell Habbestad also to write a music piece.

Prof. Hirayoshi wrote in his postcard dated 8th November last year, saying "Sorry I'm late in writing the music piece. The lyrics I've chosen are by Kitahara Hakushu on the subject of 'The first love'. The vocal part is made up of a very simple melodic line. Give me a few more days to complete it."

At last, two weeks before Mr Sparbo's arrival, the music piece by Prof. Hirayoshi reached me. I was told later that it was his last composition and that Prof. Hirayoshi had used Kitahara Hakushu's poems quite often in his early works. I now understand how profound his knowledge of Kitahara Hakushu was.

Although he did not come to the rehearsal, he rang me up to make some more arrangements in the music piece. He was anxious about the violin part if it was much too difficult for the violinist to handle. However, the violinist, Miss Yuko Aragaki did a wonderful job using all her sensitivity in her actual performance.

After the Tokyo public concert, I invited Prof. Hirayoshi onto the stage in the big applause. He kept on standing, clapping hands towards us performers with a smile. Even now, I can't forget that wonderful smile of his. As well, I can't believe that he fell into a desease from that day on and died quite recently.

I only hope that this beautiful music piece of his will be performed on many occasions in the future.

February 1999
pianist **Shuku Iwasaki**

＜The Data of the composition and its first public performance＞

Composed on the 16th of November in 1997

Commissioned by the Shuku Iwasaki "Music in Style" 1997

Tokyo's first public performance was held at the Suntory Hall on the 5th of December in 1997

Performed by Njål Sparbo, a Bass-baritone; Yuko Aragaki, a violinist;

and Shingo Nakamura together with Shuku Iwasaki, pianists

初 恋
The first love

バリトン、ヴァイオリン、ピアノ連弾のための
for Baritone, Violin, Piano 4-Hands

北原白秋 詩
poem by Hakushu Kitahara

薄らあかりにあかあかと
踊るその子はただひとり。
薄らあかりに涙して
消ゆるその子もただひとり。
薄らあかりに、おもひでに、
踊るそのひと、そのひとり。

平吉毅州 作曲
Takekuni Hirayoshi

平吉毅州（ひらよし　たけくに）

- 1936年　7月10日　神戸に生まれる。
- 1961年　東京芸術大学作曲科卒業。
  在学中、長谷川良夫に師事。
- 1962年　毎日音楽コンクール作曲部門管弦楽曲の部第1位。
- 1967年　東京芸術大学大学院作曲専攻修了。
- 1970年　昭和44年度尾高賞受賞。
- 1997年　沖縄県立芸術大学音楽学部教授。
- 1998年　5月28日　永眠。享年61。

主要作品

交響変奏曲／弦楽のためのエピタフ／ヴァイオリンとオーケストラのためのレクィエム／ギター協奏曲／独奏ティンパニーとオーケストラのための「海のある風景」／2台のマリンバのための「風の歌」／こどものためのピアノ曲集「虹のリズム」、「南の風」／混声合唱のためのスケッチ「夢」／混声合唱組曲「空に小鳥がいなくなった日」／男声合唱のための組曲「さすらいの船路」他多数。

CD

虹のリズム　ビクターエンタテインメント　VICS-61201
南の風　　　ビクターエンタテインメント　VICS-61202
　　　　　　　　　　　　　　　　　　　　他多数。

Takekuni HIRAYOSHI

- 1936　Born on July 10, in Kobe.
- 1961　Graduated from the Composition Department of Tokyo University of the Arts.
  As a student, studied under Yoshio Hasegawa.
- 1962　Received first place in the Orchestral Music Division of the Mainichi Music Competition.
- 1967　Graduated from Tokyo University of the Arts, Graduate School.
- 1970　Received the 1969 Otaka Award.
- 1997　Taught at Okinawa Prefectural University of Arts.
- 1998　Takekuni Hirayoshi died on May 28. Aged 61.

Major Works

Symphonic Variations / EPITAPH for Strings / REQUIEM for Violin and Orchestra / Guitar Concerto / "A Landscape with the Sea" for Timpani and Orchestra / "KAZE-NO-UTA" for 2 Marimbas / "RAINBOW RHYTHM" "SOUTH WIND" – the Piano Pieces for Children / "DREAM" – A Sketch for Mixed Chorus / "The Day the Birds Left the Sky" – Choral Suite for Mixed Chorus / "Wandering Voyage" – A Suite for Male Chorus. and others.

Discography

RAINBOW RHYTHM　Victor Entertainment　VICS-61201
SOUTH WIND　　　Victor Entertainment　VICS-61202
　　　　　　　　　　　　　　　　　　and others.

携帯サイトはこちら▶

出版情報&ショッピング　カワイ出版ONLINE　http://editionkawai.jp

Takekuni Hirayoshi Piano Works

ハバネラ　サンバ・カンシオン　初恋

発行日● 1999年4月1日　第1刷発行	作　曲●平吉毅州
2020年3月1日　第32刷発行	発行所●カワイ出版（株式会社 全音楽譜出版社 カワイ出版部）
	〒161-0034　東京都新宿区上落合2-13-3
	TEL.03-3227-6286　FAX.03-3227-6296
	楽譜浄書●神田屋　　　写植●フジアート
表紙装飾・デザイン●小泉卓史	印刷●保坂印刷社／平河工業社
英語訳●久保かほる	製本●リーブルテック
	© 1999 by edition KAWAI. Assigned 2017 to Zen-On Music Co., Ltd.

本書よりの転載はお断りします。
落丁・乱丁本はお取り替え致します。
本書のデザインや仕様は予告なく変更される場合がございます。

ISBN978-4-7609-0617-8